ALIGN YOUR MINDS

Seize Your Dream

Expanded Fourth Edition

ALIGN YOUR MINDS

Seize Your Dream

Thomas E. Loxley

TACHE WORKS

ALIGN YOUR MINDS: Seize Your Dream

TACHE WORKS

A specialized educational outreach type publisher. All rights are reserved. Address comments to: Thomas Loxley, 680 Canal St. - No. 402, Beaver, PA 15009. All feedback is most sincerely welcome. Your support is vital to all of our endeavors.

Manufactured in United States of America

ISBN: 9781733743099

Dewey Decimal Classification:

158 Applied Psychology

BISAC Subject Codes:

OCC019000 Inspiration and Personal Growth
PSY003000 Applied Psychology
HEA032000 Alternative Therapies
EDU032000 Leadership
POL049000 Propaganda

DEDICATION

This little book was inspired by:

Stella Loxley

A former teacher in Freedom, Pennsylvania,

and

Émile Coué

The French psychotherapist whose autosuggestion research helped millions around the world to help themselves.

CONTENTS

WELCOME

You are cordially invited to take a personal journey deep into the farthest reaches of your own minds. That is plural because we all have not just one, but two minds, one conscious and one subconscious. Any potential disagreements between them can then be a problem in anyone's psychological situation. You might see what follows as an Einstein type of thought experiment. One that has been carefully crafted to help you to better know yourself, your personal potential, and how you might achieve it.

The book is designed to promote a deliberate consideration of everything involved. It offers an easily readable layout that provides a careful flow of the information to promote its comprehension. Modern society has created a fast paced existence for everyone. In order to effectively deal with many personal issues, we need to consider how we might best then get a proper grip on them. The fine art of autosuggestion offers a vital way to deal with this. It has long worked for millions of people all over the world and should now work for you as well. The great work of the renowned psychotherapist, Emile Coue, offers us an easy way to proceed.

Various exploiters of all kinds are now literally pitting everyone against each other in order to serve many different hidden objectives. But, while modern psychological warfare imposes the will of others on you, autosuggestion can help you to take control of your own destiny. Do you remember, when you were young, how your mother cheered you up by simply getting you to sing a happy song? That was autosuggestion in its simplest form, and it is truly the most powerful tool ever known for our self-improvement. But, realizing its full potential now requires that you understand just how your two minds work, how they react to what is happening in your life, how you best influence your subconscious mind, and how you can explore your own subconscious perspective.

Autosuggestion exercises don't take very long and will not conflict with your normal activities. They involve you acting alone, in a private setting, where you can comfortably lie down and relax. They're best done just before and after sleeping. Their objective is simply to help you to know yourself and the realization of your own potential. *Align Your Minds* now offers you a practical guide that can help you to properly do all of this.

INTRODUCTION

My Navy career was launched in 1961 in the midst of the Cold War with the old Soviet Union. I had just graduated from Case Tech's new R&D type Engineering Science program, which was a formal collaboration with Caltech and MIT. It was designed to produce broad based engineers who were primed to explore some radically innovative problem solutions. With the Navy, I had become aware of new psychological warfare developments occurring after World War II. That is now the basis of this work, which is dedicated to my mother and the special bond we shared. We both knew what we wanted to do early in life. She was a natural teacher who loved kids and I was a natural engineer who saw every problem as a personal challenge. Few people today seem to be quite that lucky.

While diamonds may be fine gems, they used to be ordinary lumps of coal. All it took was time and pressure to turn an ordinary lump of coal into an incredible diamond. Your own potential is much the same. Whereas a diamond depends upon huge geological forces, your fate is now up to you. If you should fail to recognize that reality, your own precious life force can easily be wasted serving the predatory elements that are now literally all around you. Everyone really needs to be their own biggest cheerleader. Success is just that simple and the tools that you need were all developed long ago by our evolving human civilization. It is high time that you learned how to use them for yourself. It doesn't matter how old you are today.

In his book, *The Lonely Crowd,* sociologist David Riesman saw society being divided into inner and other directed types of people. While the inner directed people took active charge of their lives, other directed people were dependent on others to define who they were, how they should think, and what they might do. The shape and nature of any particular society then reflected the effects of the interaction of these two basic groups. The other directed type of person inevitably seems to become entrapped by their growing responsibilities. These are naturally related to practical concerns such as education, employment, marriage, homes, children, health, etc.

The famed Greek philosopher, Socrates, had advised everyone that their primary mission in life was to know their self. However, today's child is now born into a chaotic world, filled with sensual inputs that are all now clamoring for their undivided attention. It is estimated the average American parent has only one or two minutes of daily conversation with their very own children. Those children then often feel that they are literally on their own when it comes to sorting out any ulterior motives of the people around them.

Life is like a great river of experience that never stops for anyone. It is up to you to define how you will ride that stream with all of its many challenges and surprises. A ride that you are surely free to perceive as one of toil and pain or endless wonder. Your personal happiness is then derived from your own inner perspective on life itself. No matter the circumstances, you can freely choose to make either a heaven or hell out of it. History now literally abounds with seemingly impossible stories of people who started out with virtually nothing and succeeded anyway.

When early humans first roamed the African savannas, they lived in family groups as simple hunter gatherers. Their population was small and scattered according to the natural resources that they required. Their migration into villages, towns, and cities began with the development of simple agriculture and animal husbandry. This gathering of families then depended upon their increasing ability to communicate and cooperate. The grunts, whistles, and screams of apes evolved into words and speech allowing the proper transfer of ever more complicated facts, ideas, and observations. At some critical points in our human history, major events are seen to have occurred when our society dramatically improved. This may have coincided with development of our growing communication ability enabling greater leadership and collaboration. The increasing pride in such accomplishments is then expected to have generated even grander developments.

I believe that in successfully leading your life, there is much to learn from the age old lessons of human leadership. Indeed, leadership was born out of the necessities of group survival and the social nature of our species. Starting with individual families, it grew to include the need of clans, tribes, cities, nations, and eventually the world. The burden of early leadership was naturally defined by our basic physical, defensive, and spiritual requirements. Food, shelter, safety, and the awesome power of nature were always then centermost on their minds. Their survival literally depended on the emergence of leaders who could eventually transform their growing population into a potentially flourishing nation.

The clan chieftains, religious shamans, and defensive warriors faced the same dilemma as those today in their need for proper support. Meaningful workers, believers, and defenders were critical to group survival. This forced leaders to become experts in the fine art of attracting, motivating, and controlling the people that they required. Failed leaders then did not often survive. The successful ones then came to represent a circle of experts on these matters who prized the tricks of their trade. They had actively sought to learn how to psychologically control their tribal members. Their biggest discoveries were then kept secret from the very people that they affected the most.

Early leaders were then initially limited to direct face to face communication with their followers. This was later expanded by the written word. Our modern development of radio, movies, television, and Internet have now created a whole new world. Along with this came a really intense study of the psychology involved in manipulating the basic thought processes of the individual human being. In the Cold War, this pitted the leading world forces against each other in what is called psychological warfare. This then often included propaganda and disinformation campaigns that we targeted at citizens on our own side as well as the enemy. It involved the exclusive training of military officers in these arts. Training which they took home with them when they left the military. Now, it seems that these dark arts were often wrongly employed, against their own unsuspecting neighbors, in order to wrongly make money or seize political power.

Whether you realize it or not, you now live in an age of rampant psychological warfare, often called psywar. If you think that it is not deeply affecting you, then you are really either a liar or a fool. The liars know they are wrongly profiting from this truly exploitive situation, while the fools are willfully ignorant of what is happening all around them. Their own situational ignorance is now being actively shaped by all of our modern social pressures and distractions. Indeed, most Americans can now speak of obscure sports statistics much more readily than they can any aspect of their own national history. Ask them a simple philosophic question and they often only echo some inane propaganda.

Today's modern computer and electronic developments gave us the Internet, which has proved to be both a fantastic new resource and offensive meddler in our personal lives. Handy cellphones have literally allowed us to tap into information anywhere on anything. Ask it how to do something and a dozen YouTube videos provide instant instruction. Social media allow you to get the latest news as well as build new friendships and associations all over the world. You can literally buy anything or even get a college education online. However, much of the information on the Internet is often untrue or twisted to serve some hidden agenda. Many online sites now currently exist simply to spread propaganda and disinformation that is aimed at manipulating your thinking to serve some secret objective. Your own most intimate confidences and exposures may now be stolen to then entertain or enrich some dark interests at your expense. A new personal wariness has become essential to your Internet survival.

As an engineering scientist who has observed the unfolding of this situation over fifty years, I feel that I should honestly try to give you my own personal perspective on our modern world. First of all, you need to appreciate that we all possess two minds, one conscious and one subconscious. This will give you a much better appreciation of all of the little tricks that other people are now employing to secretly impose their personal self-serving dogmas deep into your own mind. In order to counteract it, you must then literally design a personal agenda that your subconscious mind really believes to be far more important. Its harmonious repetition can then actually help you to overcome many bad habits or destructive ideas. Visualizing your personal objectives as if they already exist can also help to assure you of their ultimate realization. Your own subconscious muscular reflexes might even offer invaluable feedback on the relationship of your two minds. These fundamental skills and knowledge can then encourage a practical, project oriented, perspective on life that can offer you some real satisfaction as you grow into an ever better understanding of yourself and whatever you really want to do.

YOUR TWO MINDS

The human brain is physically divided into two halves as shown. Our left and right hemispheres then promote two very distinct views of the world.

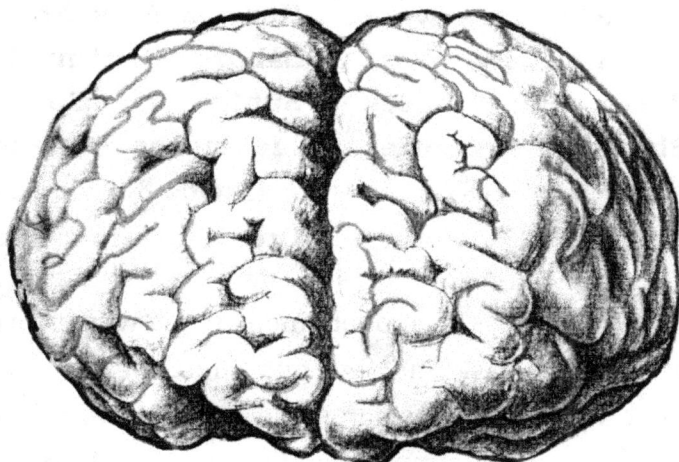

THE HUMAN BRAIN

This basic separation is a vital aspect of our personal behavior. It is likened to our thinking processes being divided into two minds inside of one body. The one is objective and conscious, while the other is subjective and subconscious. Their individual attributes are then seen as follows:

11

C O N S C I O U S (Left Brain)	**SUBCONSCIOUS** (Right Brain)
Rational Executive	Emotional Servant
Cautious Appraisal	Believes Anything
Purpose & Principle	Dreams & Fantasy
Restrictive Memory	Total Living Recall
Space/Time Aware	Here & Now Focus
Needs Daily Rest	Labors Continually
Basic Five Senses	Subliminal Senses
Physical Activities	Ideomotor Reflexes
Math & Sciences	Artistic & Musical
Writing & Speaking	Creates & Imagines

We witness such phenomena when we perform a repetitive task and find our mind goes on auto pilot while we consider some personal problem. Hypnosis is a simple way of tapping into our subconscious mind. However, left brain dominant engineers, like me, are then naturally harder to hypnotize than right brain artists. Our conscious and subconscious minds are natural parts of the human nervous system. While one undertakes our objective thinking activities, the other takes on all of those boring repetitive tasks of operating our heart, lungs, digestion, etc. Should you ever repeatedly consider any idea or perform any task, your subconscious mind will consider making it a part of your habitual character. Habits are thus far easier to form than they are to ever suppress. Our subconscious mind tends to hold especially tightly onto anything entered with real emotion. This is clearly seen in cases of Post-Traumatic Stress Disorder (PTSD) reported by military veterans.

Our conscious mind is the boss while the subconscious is its loyal servant. Although our conscious mind can rationally consider any idea or situation, our subconscious mind is apt to respond dramatically to any inputs that trigger its emotional sensitivity. The problem is that our subconscious mind does not care if something is true or false. It simply takes its orders from any repetitive suggestions you make. This makes our subconscious mind extremely vulnerable to our repeating any senseless idea or malicious gossip that isn't properly dismissed by our own conscious analysis. Both roles demand serious training and experience to do well.

Our subconscious mind can only reason in a simple deductive fashion. It will then use all of its accumulated inputs to formulate self-serving type dogmas for all occasions. It is utterly bewildered by any challenges to its opinion. Even worse, our subconscious mind can demonstrate a childlike aversion to being told 'not' to do anything. Tell it not to and it may well want to give it a try. Don't waste your time telling yourself what is wrong. Instead, focus on telling yourself what you really want. Our conscious mind rationally determines our goals, focus, and values, while our subconscious seems to conjure up all of our vain dreams and fantasies from its vast warehouse of past experience.

The memory capacity of the two minds is apportioned much like that in a personal computer. While our conscious working memory is limited so it can be really nimble, the long term storage of our subconscious mind is truly enormous. Indeed, it has the potential capability of recalling every single sensual experience in our entire lives. Modern criminal investigators are now utilizing hypnosis to tap into the subconscious memories of witnesses to retrieve some obscure details of a crime, like the license number of a getaway car.

However, your subconscious mind cannot delete anything. You can only suppress any bad habits or thoughts by repeatedly imposing some attractive replacements that your subconscious mind is then convinced are far more important. Psychologists often use hypnosis to seek out any hidden memories that may then be causing people emotional problems. Our subconscious mind is extremely protective of our psychological wellbeing and may often try to suppress certain experiences that it deems to be too dangerous for us to recall. These are often memories that it believes we are simply ill prepared to handle emotionally at that particular moment.

While our conscious mind may take some rational action to deal with any situation, our subconscious just records everything that happens. While the conscious mind makes us properly aware of our place in the wider world and history, our subconscious mind lives in the here and now. Our conscious concerns over attending an early appointment can then literally program our subconscious to wake us up, like an alarm clock. The subconscious mind is constantly working to keep us alive, avoid pain, seek pleasure, and satisfy our need to propagate the species. Since our subconscious literally has no concept of the future, and doesn't even know the difference between imagination and reality, it can often work tirelessly on granting our visualized hopes as if they are already fulfilled. This fantastic property can then often help us to accomplish seeming miracles, fueled by our own visualizations, affirmations, and emotional emphasis. They say that whatever you can focus on and visualize in your imagination, you can then come to realize. Your imagination is far more effective than your will power in obtaining whatever you might desire.

In order to keep our heart and other vital organs running properly, our subconscious mind can never take a break. Nonetheless, our bodies go through daily cycles of restful behavior that then allow it to be refreshed and renewed. This is denoted by brainwave frequencies that are recorded on an electroencephalograph (EEG) in the beta, alpha, theta, and delta frequency modes shown below:

CYCLES PER SECOND (Hz)

Beta	Alpha	Theta	Delta
12-20	8-12	5-7	0.5-4

Beta is our normal alert behavior at 12-20 cycles per second or Hertz (Hz). Alpha is light sleep or meditation, where the rapid eye movement

(REM) phenomenon occurs, at 8-12 Hz. Theta is deep sleep at 5-7 Hz, while delta is very deep sleep at 0.5-4 Hz, where the body is said to repair itself. Our suggestibility increases quite markedly upon entering an alpha state. This is something we can often do simply by closing our eyes. Another way to assist our entering any given brain state is called brainwave entrainment. This simply involves using acoustic, light, or tactile stimulation of a given frequency. It is often done simply by listening to an audio CD containing that particular frequency while relaxing. The binaural beat phenomenon uses stereo headphones to impose one frequency on one side and a second frequency on the other. The brain will then acquire a frequency equal to the difference between them. If one is 30 Hz and the other is 20 Hz, the brainwave will be entrained at an alpha state of 10 Hz. These phenomena are related to those situations where we often find ourselves tapping our feet to some musical rhythm or being drawn to a particular piece of music. The sleeping alpha and theta modes are ideal for implanting your personal aspirations, special needs, and visualizations deep in your subconscious. This is best done just before we go to sleep, so that the subconscious mind can then be encouraged to focus on them overnight.

Our senses of vision, hearing, touch, taste, and smell form our conscious view of the world around us. The subtler concepts of intuition, subliminal, and psychic abilities are all part of our subconscious. We have all heard about subliminal advertising, where illustrations are flashed so fast in front of us that they simply don't register in our conscious mind. They are then, nonetheless, somehow detected by our subconscious, tempting us to buy whatever they portray. Many advertisers have now invested heavily in research aimed at finding new ways of triggering such impulsive purchases. This subliminal sensitivity then helps us recognize the threatening body language of a potential adversary or the come hither glance of a potential mate. It is a major part of our subconscious protective system that is aimed at keeping us alive, avoiding pain and seeking pleasure. This remarkable ability plays a big role in shaping any potential encounters with our subconscious mind.

It is also why any related exercises should be conducted where you can relax and be alone. Your psyche just cannot help picking up any skeptical vibrations from the people around you. This can then act to suppress any subconscious cooperation. This is why many public psychic demonstrations tend to fail in the presence of any skepticism. Just think of your own subconscious mind as a shy child who literally refuses to perform in front of any strangers. If you really want to personally see any good results, you must then suppress any skepticism and make a sincere effort to believe that this truly amazing phenomenon might just work for you.

While our conscious mind directs our body's physical activity, any athletic skill is rooted in its practiced training where our subconscious mind is programmed to assist us in the performance of a particular sport. Our ideomotor reflex movements are very subtle subconscious physical motions that can offer us a rudimentary form of communication between our conscious and subconscious minds. This is mental driven muscular action where a given thought causes a detectable physical reaction, without any conscious control. Investigated by the noted scientist, Michael Faraday, this amazing natural phenomenon is behind such things as automatic writing, water dowsing, and similar activities. Using a simple pendulum on a string, its movement can be amplified to offer subconscious YES or NO responses to some simple conscious inquiries into its particular body of knowledge. However, this should never be seen as lending itself, in any way, to telling fortunes, reading people's minds, or talking to your dead relatives.

Your own natural left or right brain dominance plays a vital role in our personal lives as well as that in our society. Left brain dominated people tend to lean toward structural organization and systematic type analysis. These tend to include mathematicians, scientists, and accountants. Right brain types then lean toward free expression and natural harmony. These will typically include poets, musicians, and painters. Although both groups also share all of the qualities listed before, their left and right brain proclivities can make life quite interesting. It is to be generally hoped that all of these diverse personalities will then harmonically complement each other in positive ways that then make for a better world.

ALIGN YOUR MINDS

Our conscious mind is accountable for our ability to write and speak in ways that others can readily understand. The subconscious mind then adds that creative and imaginative significance to our everyday communications that make it a vital part of our life's story. The human mind really seems to appreciate constructive inputs that lend themselves to forming attractive and cohesive sorts of personal stories. This is a big part of our own psychic perspective. Your own subconscious growth may then depend upon you providing guidance that helps to build your own personal history and philosophy. Winning the wholehearted cooperation of your personal conscious and subconscious minds demands an attractive storyline that really serves your aspirations. Think of this as being your big chance to construct a personal legacy and future that can really suit your own talent and ambition. Politicians do this all the time, so why shouldn't you? Don't ever hesitate to make it as big, bold, and attractive as you desire. This very process can then set your own subconscious mind to work on defining all of the practical steps that you need to take in order to turn your dreams into reality. Don't ever doubt its ability to do that.

SECRETS & DOGMA

You should realize that much of this research has been done by leaders who were seeking ever better control over you. This included military, government, religious, and academic groups that are responsible for our survival. Modern industry then introduced capitalism into our society. Unlike the others, corporations exist only to profit from selling various goods and services. This led to advertising and public relations groups that are bent upon coaxing us to buy whatever they have to offer. However, like all too many of our human endeavors, its profiteering has become ever more obsessive. Many fear that modern capitalism is far more of a money worshipping cult than an economic system. While free enterprise, communism, and socialism were all designed to serve the interests of society, capitalism often seems to be fixated upon creating a new, greed driven, type of aristocracy.

Political systems, like Sweden's democratic socialism, allow voters to decide whether aspects of its society are deemed to be common interests or suitable for free enterprise. The top one percent of Americans now owns much of the nation and there is literally no end to the things that money can buy. Like ugly medieval aristocrats, they are often seen as deceitfully imposing a menacing modern economic serfdom on their less fortunate neighbors. This has involved replacing America's former military draft with a new pro-corporate type of voluntary service. The U.S. Supreme Court recently even ruled that corporations have all the same rights as any citizens. This clearly undermined American democracy by empowering its corporate lobbyists to literally buy elected officials, who are then obligated to serve their selfish profiteering interests.

American society now clearly reflects all of the accumulated psychological baggage of our ever advancing civilization. Its territorial interests are rooted in our early hunter gatherer days of living off the land. Families then took the boundaries of their food and water supplies very seriously. Markers were put down to warn off any potential intruders. These subsequently evolved into family crests and mottoes that helped to bond members together. Families merged into clans that merged into tribes and then into nations. Distinctive clothing led to flags and other totems that helped to build a group identity and distinguish them from any foreigners.

Territorial conflicts easily resulted in warfare when the local subsistence was at stake. This violence grew from hand-to-hand combat into that between ever larger groups, depending upon the population and the level of technology that was involved. While combat was always a real part of our human nature, the ever evolving weaponry made it an increasingly deadly proposition for anyone to be caught on the ever expanding battlefield.

Early leaders studied all of the considerations involved in handling people. They saw that it helped to get their attention if you fed and entertained them somehow. People with empty bellies didn't pay serious attention to anyone. This became known as bread and circus type leadership. Rhythmic drums and group chanting, along with late night bonfires, helped to set the stage. Leaders soon learned the importance of repeating their message, and that it was most effective if the people went to bed with it still fresh in their minds. Such occasions then naturally evolved into regular festivals that helped to build popular interest and anticipation. The leadership hierarchy similarly expanded with their population, and it continually sought to build a tribal history, real or imagined, that entrenched their authority and helped to build a special type of group identity. War was all too common and the winners always shaded their history to suit themselves.

The first writing system may now be over six thousand years old. Yet, much of Earth's population was virtually kept illiterate until recent centuries. Literacy was then a class privilege that distinguished the anointed few from the general population. Any mass communication was vocally transmitted in terms that the masses could readily understand. Such meetings then usually sought to produce some cooperative action related to the local resources, resolving internal squabbles, building some new project, raising an army, dealing with disasters, or levying taxation. Local storytellers regularly memorized and recited any official proclamations, insuring that everyone was properly informed.

The invention of the printing press posed a very real threat to any leaders who were quite content with the existing status quo. The rapid proliferation of printed materials have encouraged many major educational movements. And those newly educated citizens demanded more sophisticated leadership in virtually all sectors of society. Public libraries have now made the printed word available to many people for their personal self-improvement. These vital opportunities facilitated numerous political movements which then posed more challenges for the existing leadership.

However, local education opportunities still vary greatly around the world. Modern democracies generally support a uniform, secular, public type education. Yet, in many places, the only education still exists in highly partisan schools that are then designed to serve some particular ideology. Back in Nazi Germany, Adolf Hitler successfully modified all of the schools to obediently serve his Nazi Party. And we all remember how that turned out.

Disciplinary codes were created and efforts made to turn the local beliefs into law. However, arguments over sensitive issues are often very difficult to resolve to everyone's satisfaction. Dogma emerged as the answer. It was then declared that something was the 'final' answer. That subject was then dispensed with so others could be entertained. But, contrary opinions seldom die quietly. Wise men have long warned everyone that the potential downfall of any democratic government lay in our seemingly insatiable human appetite for vain, self-serving, types of dogma.

ALIGN YOUR MINDS

The community at large is often unaware of all the controversies that are part of its governance. This process is then invariably built on the secrecy that the leadership deems to be necessary in order to preserve peace in the community. Such secrecy is really nothing new to human relations. Siblings, friends, lovers, parents, and groups of all sorts rarely tell each other everything. Our subconscious mind believes it is often best to suppress certain unpleasant sorts of experiences. Such secrecy was of modest impact back when Earth's human population was under one billion, and most people then lived in rural communities. However, the population is now over eight billion, and modern technology has driven people into crowded cities, where many are at their wits ends. Many now feel lost in the shuffle, with their lives reduced to being little more than numbers on some vast government registry. A recent study showed that many Americans couldn't even see how they could find $400 to contend with a minor emergency. This dilemma appears to be greatly aggravated in our super capitalistic America, which seems to be surrendering more and more control to its greediest captains of industry.

Two world wars have now shown the enormous profits available from such deadly global conflicts. My own career showed me that the real winners in any modern war, hot or cold, are its corporate war profiteers. General Smedley Butler, a decorated war hero in the U.S. Marine Corps, tried to tell us that. However, few Americans appeared to have cared. President Eisenhower also warned us about the growing dictatorial influence of our vast military industrial complex. But again, no one ever really seemed to care. The common man has invariably seemed to be far too absorbed in all of their inane vanities to ever see the impact of that harsh reality. Some now like to fantasize that somehow America actually 'won' the Cold War.

The New York Times estimated the Cold War cost us $5.5 trillion in 1996 dollars. However, this is really rather deceptive. The conflict evolved as a continuation of World War II, and benefitted from an American public and military industrial complex that were fully war oriented. There was no major drawdown of the military forces, as had occurred after World War I. Profiteers then eagerly sought the next war, where our casualties might be limited, while their profits were made utterly irresistable.

ALIGN YOUR MINDS

Few Americans realize the role that Nazi Germany had played in the development of our own creeping corporate fascism. They are unaware of the major role that Wall Street and American industrialists had then played in the rise of Adolf Hitler. Of course, our sanitized corporate fascism has long disavowed the racial imperialism involved in Hitler's demise.

While corporate profits were regulated back in WWI, such controls were eliminated after WWII. The Cold War became a profiteer's dream come true. WWII also created secret windfalls from U.S. seizure of Germany and Japan's stolen booty from conquered lands. This treasure, worth trillions of dollars, was then seen as a huge secret slush fund that was used to finance many covert operations. It is also believed that it may have helped to fund the Marshall Plan, used to rebuild wartorn Europe.

A truly self-serving concept of national security emerged to classify and cover-up any corruption. War tactics and weapons research continued at full speed after WWII. Unacknowledged Special Access Projects were created to hide Black projects from public scrutiny. These consumed huge fortunes, while undertaking many tasks that the country had often publicly disavowed. Most people don't know

now where the truth leaves off and fiction begins regarding such things as covert wars, FEMA and immigrant concentration camps, secret prisons, cyber warfare, domestic spying, mind control, UFOs, ancient aliens, cattle mutilation, climate change, HAARP, chem-trails, toxic hazards, etc. The CIA often ridicules credible witnesses as wild conspiracy theorists, while forcing any military personnel involved into signing Non-Disclosure Agreements. It's believed to secretly expand its budget with counterfeit super dollars spent abroad. And it is accused of using military air transport to smuggle illegal drugs into the U.S. for distribution by some of the worst elements of organized crime.

Armchair warriors often forget that there are two sides to any conflict and an adversary should never be assumed to be impotent or ignorant of their dilemma. Nothing really motivates creative genius or great heroism more than your own personal survival. In the Korean War, our experts were shocked when Russian guns and planes proved far better and cheaper than our own. American weapons have often seemed to be designed more to maximize their corporate profits than they are for battlefield safety or effectiveness.

Both the purchase and operating costs of our latest crop of warplanes are truly astronomical.

Russia has now launched a new hybrid type of war designed to cheaply destroy our democratic elections, civil society, and national economy. This war by other means is no small matter and Americans ignore it at their peril. Adolf Hitler had ingeniously exploited his new media of movies and radio. Now, Vladimir Putin is exploiting the Internet and social media in a covert campaign of sabotage and psychological warfare that has caught most Americans naively unaware.

Serious investigations show 21 trillion dollars to be unaccounted for in the U.S. Department of Defense, with yet another 2 trillion dollars in its Department of Housing and Urban Development. This money is seen as being used to finance various Black programs. The Pentagon refuses to do any serious auditing, because it apparently doesn't know where to begin. Such defense expenditures notoriously create far fewer jobs for U.S. workers, compared to money being spent on roads, bridges, parks, schools, hospitals, etc. Today's derelict American infrastructure is undeniable proof of this monstrous political corruption and wanton deceit.

Thomas E. Loxley

The American taxpayers surely deserve an honest, detailed, and full accounting of what they are getting for their money. What can the American people think when no bigshots ever went to prison for having caused the economic collapse of 2008? The growing national debt has greatly depreciated the value of America's dollar. This now threatens to undermine it as the world's reserve currency, further harming the nation's economic stability. A potential trade war with China and coronavirus pandemic then menaced everyone's health care, living costs, and job security.

America's persistent racism, born out of slavery, illustrates the destructive impact of psychological warfare. The European colonial settlement of the U.S. had given many aspiring aristocrats control over vast tracts of land. That land and climate were often ideal for raising valuable, labor intensive, crops like cotton and sugar cane. The potential availability of slave labor was then deemed to be ideal for maximizing the profitability of those big plantations. Their output also represented great potential wealth for the related industrial areas, where large textile mills and food processors then built their fortunes on the backs of African slaves.

Fortunes which had provided wide employment for anyone fortunate enough to be born white.

The upstanding European settlers, who profited mightily, felt obligated to offer some adequate reasoning for having enslaved their fellow man. Nonsensical studies then purported to prove white superiority. Biblical references were also produced to justify the practice. Those studies were often endorsed by major religious bodies. This evil dogma caused many widespread racial atrocities. When it then managed to endure for four centuries, its psychological embedding became hard to ignore. This evil practice was eventually condemned by many of the world's leading civilized nations. However, America was one of the last to do this, and it then culminated in one of the bloodiest civil wars in human history.

The resulting aftermath left many people indelibly affected by racist rationalizations that they consider comforting and hard to abandon. However, the world at large is now relentlessly becoming a meritocracy, where education, hard work, and experience are seen as the keys to national prosperity. While progressive nations sought to defuse such racial tension by providing education and employment opportunities, they were irresponsibly allowed to fester in the United States. If it should now allow white racist extremist militias and law enforcement to undermine national peace, it could well encourage key members of its highly technical work force to seek safer refuge abroad. A dilemma that has now been made all the worse by America's debacle in handling the coronavirus pandemic, when over a million people perished.

Every time we now buy anything, voice our opinions, establish relationships, or record our big personal accomplishments, it is being monitored by various enterprising or analytic entities. While some seem harmless, even beneficial, others seek to tap our bank account or natural vulnerabilities for their selfish benefit. Ads now routinely appear on your phone and computer that are designed just for you. Your personal and professional data, purchasing interests, and financial data can all be secretly sold to anyone. This can then allow them to target the intimate aspects of your life for devious objectives. Literally everything about you is now seen as fair game and could allow criminal entry into your personal life via cyber manipulation. We all need to be aware of a growing number of potential threats.

Individually, we must determine how to best deal with all of the information and responsibilities that are impacting everyone. Some may choose to follow the path of willful ignorance over the difficult search for truth. Propagandists, using secrecy and dogma, are constantly working to demonize many fine options deserving our serious consideration. However, even highly educated scientists often discard any facts that challenge their accepted views of the world. And many religious people still dogmatically question the idea of natural evolution. Some insist that the world is only six thousand years old. It can clearly be difficult for anyone to keep an open mind in our modern world.

There are still many ways for you to help yourself to better deal with life's dilemmas. It is important for everyone to maximize and define their own personal options in setting their goals and priorities. Are your present associates and situation really compatible with your aspirations? What steps should you seriously consider taking, right now, in order to improve your own situation and hopes for tomorrow? Have you ever tried to actually lay out your very own plan on paper? Your personal future is really in your own hands.

Thomas E. Loxley

THE NEW DARK SIDE

While many hazards in life are readily detectable, modern technology has introduced new invisible threats for everyone. The reality of mind control, utilizing electromagnetic radiation, was a result of secret research conducted during the Cold War. Modern radar was then critical in detecting any attacking enemy ships or planes. And in order to insure its safety, the radiation effects on the human body had to be very carefully examined. Its noted effects on the human brain then invited secret mind manipulation research in both the USA and USSR. Much of this work focused on the obvious ability of certain radio frequencies to resonate deep inside the human brain. Testing at Montauk, New York, then exposed numerous subjects to different radar frequencies and signal strength in various scenarios. They showed that some low frequency pulses of high frequency radiation had significant behavioral effects. It seemed to be especially effective when combined in a controlled environmental type of situation. Both willing and unwilling volunteers were supposedly employed to explore some tactical applications, yielding a number of horror stories.

Their big discovery was that a low frequency pulsation of a particular radar frequency seemed to literally shut down our conscious mind. It was like some powerful new kind of electronic hypnotism, that no one could resist. This meant they could then freely manipulate the information flowing into our subconscious mind for any number of objectives. This resulted in projects like the Lida Machine in Russia and MK-ULTRA in America. North Korean interrogators of U.S. POWs are said to have used the Lida Machine to then talk them into confessing to a variety of war crimes. The CIA is said to use similar technology to implant bizarre memories into U.S. servicemen. This then undermined their ability to ever disclose the truth about its covert activities, by provoking their impulsive insistance of having been based on the Moon or Mars. This destroyed their credibility with a naive news media, which then rejected everything they had to say. Although the U.S. Senate Church Committee exposed many of these activities back in 1975, little was ever done to fully expose, stop, or control them. No one was ever prosecuted and there is no assurance at all that they are still not going on today. Indeed, this research appears to have been steadily advanced.

Manufacturers were employed to refine these developments into practical electronic equipment that was made more readily available. The initial use of electronic hypnosis was highly restricted to military and intelligence operations. But, as its use and design became more attractive, it is believed that its covert civilian uses became irresistable to those seeking special advantage over any adversary. They are now seen to be readily incorporated into the ceilings of most any auditorium, church, or hall. They offer to give most any message being offered a new persuasive influence that could be irresistable. Unscrupulous ministers might readily draw new mega-flocks of financially supportive worshippers away from their traditional churches. Politicians, entertainers, and hustlers of all sorts could all find it very profitable. Such radar hypnosis stimulators are now said to be secretly available to a very restricted clientele, who don't want you to know that such things even exist. However, new pocket sized detectors of pulsed radiation are available that can now alert anyone to their use. It is also expected that some local volunteer investigative groups might become available that could help to expose anyone utilizing them to bilk the public.

As if the covert development of pulsed radar hypnosis was not bad enough, modern computer technology offers artificial intelligence, called AI. It appears to be potentially capable of learning how to do almost anything so as to eventually put most everyone out of a job. AI can learn how to write and talk just like you. It can then portray you saying embarassing or incriminating things that you would never say. It can even use innocent pictures of you to create realistic videos of you doing virtually anything. This might even then be coordinated with the use of pulsed radar hypnosis. It could well facilitate a new means of dangerous mega-mob motivation to serve the evil objectives of some emerging political plutocrat. And who knows where that might lead in today's politics.

Given the growing public disgust with the U.S. Supreme Court, it could only be a matter of time before its AI replacement is formally proposed. Indeed, AI offers to be a far more reliable way of digesting and interpreting all of the vast legal history of the United States. Surely, it could easily avoid many of the recent revocations of established human rights and the shocking personnel scandals of the current Chief Justice Roberts' court.

Thomas E. Loxley

PROMOTING YOURSELF

Emile Coue was a pharmacist in the French city of Troyes, who discovered the amazing psychological phenomenon now known as the placebo effect. While serving thousands of patients, he noted that any medicine seemed to work much better if it was accompanied by confident affirmations that 'it' was surely just the right one for them. Around 1920, he opened a popular 'free' clinic in the city of Nancy, where he practiced a motivational type psychotherapy that he called autosuggestion. Over the years, he successfully helped millions of people all over the world. This simple technique fulfilled a variety of personal needs. While some sought the cure for some physical or mental malady, others sought his help in gratifying their frustrated life ambitions. His work was endorsed by many authorities, and affected many conditions that few saw as psychological.

Coue saw our subconscious mind as the conscientious librarian of our own accumulated personal experiences as well as regulating every aspect of our body. He believed it might then be encouraged to help sort out, define, and correct whatever was necessary to meet many people's objectives. Emile Coue sought to help everyone to obtain what he called self-mastery, where their conscious will and subconscious imagination are made to effectively work together in order to serve their own best interests. Autosuggestion helped some patients to see that half the job of overcoming many distressing health issues was often psychological and that autosuggestion might offer them real relief, if not a cure. Autosuggestion helped others to refocus their personal efforts and attention on systematically attacking all of the steps that were then involved in attaining some special personal objective in their lives. *Coue routinely encouraged all his patients to also seek out any appropriate help that might be available from conventional medicine.*

I believe that anyone wanting to make progress using autosuggestion needs to visualize their subconscious mind as a sort of twin brother or sister who then lives inside of them. You must consciously accept your responsibility to train and supervise your subconscious mind to serve your highest aspirations. Your subconscious mind trusts you to tell it what is right and wrong as well as what you want to do. It loves you and takes its obligation to serve and protect you seriously. It demands and deserves your respect. If you do not take that responsibility seriously, you could pay a high price in the form of all sorts of bad habits, addictions, failures, and breakdowns. Moreover, constructively working with your own subconscious mind can well offer you some really attractive potential benefits. You are literally a team where your individual natures offer to complement each other in some rather fantastic and rewarding ways.

I propose that you conduct a brief exercise twice a day, every day, before you go to sleep at night and again before getting up in the morning. This simply consists of the following three steps:

1. Physical Relaxation Ritual

2. Deep Breathing Meditation

3. General Autosuggestions

The first step involves creating your own personal ritual of relaxing by yourself, alone. This should always be done in some private area where you can really make yourself comfortable. The task of working with your subconscious mind demands that you try to banish any doubts and skepticism in the idea. It has worked for millions of others and there is no reason why it will not work for you. This is not a group activity and observers are not permitted. It may be done indoors or outdoors. You might like to play soft background music or listen to one of the new brain entrainment CDs. Lie down on a bed or sofa where you can fully stretch out. A simple sort of relaxation exercise usually consists of individually tensing and relaxing each of your muscles, starting down at your feet and ending up at your neck. I like to finish by fixing my eyes on an imaginary spot on the ceiling, that is located directly above my head.

The second step aims to reawaken your awareness of the importance of the two little words: *I am*. You literally need to take them into your very soul. Until you let them reverberate throughout your being, you will not truly exist. Next time you see a young child, puppy, kitten, or other animal, note the enthusiasm with which they explore their new world. Their every move reflects the sheer joy of being alive. That glorious song is then summed up in the two words: *I am!*

You knew them well enough as a child. However, adults often get distracted by life's brutal realities. If you now want to make any real progress, you must relearn and embrace the role those words play in your personal aspirations. Now, use them as a sort of mantra in a deep breathing type of meditation. After closing your eyes, take a deep breath, hold it briefly, then exhale slowly while saying: *I am*. Doing ten to twenty of these deep breathing meditations can help you to develop a suggestible alpha brain state.

The final step involves reciting Emile Coue's famous general autosuggestion. This is done while clearly envisioning your own personal objectives as having been 'already' fulfilled as you turn them over to your subconscious mind. It may be a cure for a physical or emotional problem, the vision of you completing some special project, a successful anticipated business venture, or virtually anything. The idea is to then hold that picture clearly in your imagination before repeating Coue's affirmation twenty times, with emphasis on the words: *I am*. I use twenty beads, strung in a loop, to simplify the counting. Emile Coue's healing affirmation goes as follows:

**Every day, in every way,
I am getting better and better.**

With our alteration for general use being:

**Every day, step by step,
I am now bound to succeed.**

Keep it short and simple for the maximum effect. Simultaneously submitting your specific personal desire then makes it the night long focus of your subconscious mind. This literally charges it with assessing your concerns and producing some beneficial results. It helped many people to sort out and galvanize their strength to overcome a shortcoming or distressing illness. And it helped others to better understand all of the steps involved in accomplishing their grand personal objectives. Emile Coue's instruction was crafted to help you establish a sound working relationship with your own subconscious mind. It does this with an appreciation of just how you can communicate most effectively. He believed you should never use any complex vocabulary in this critical process. His simple affirmation was based on a lifetime of experience. Its design was also shaped by his need to serve the widely varying desires of the thousands of patients and students who had eagerly crowded into his large home and garden on the Rue Jeanne d'Arc.

After you've done Emile Coue's repetitions for a while, you may well experience what I call the 'Gotya' signal. This is an unconscious halting of the repetitions, where you suddenly find yourself to be in the middle of an unrelated dream. I see it as a sort of self-hypnotic state that has simply been induced by doing the repetitions. I like to visualize my subconscious as saying: *"Okay! I got the message and I will do what I can!"* I see this as confirming that we have established real contact. However, if you ever consciously anticipate that this should occur, you can rest assured that it just won't happen. Emile Coue had called this the law of reverse effect. If you ever try to consciously will your subconscious into doing almost anything, your subconscious won't do it. It is then imperative that you strive to silence your conscious mind as much as possible so that your subconscious mind is then free to act. This is always best done just before you go to sleep at night, and just before you get up in the morning.

You might also want to reinforce your regular repetitions of Coue's autosuggestion by repeating it throughout the day, to yourself or out loud, as often as you want. If you truly seek to overcome any bad habit, it is important that you literally bury it with the assertive introduction of a more attractive one. Your subconscious mind will then attempt to assess your priorities based upon the repeated use of these simple affirmations, your vivid visualizations, and the emotional emphasis that they are given.

In dealing with everyday aches and pains, patients were advised to gently rub the area that's involved while repeating the phrase: "*It passes.*" His treatment for insomnia involved reciting the phrase: "*I am going to sleep.*" The objective was to monotonously drone yourself to sleep while keeping your conscious mind as quiet as possible. Many cases of limb paralysis often persist after medical authorities believe them to be cured. Emile Coue then overcame their mental persistence by getting the patient to simply repeat: "*I can walk*, talk, etc." He routinely produced serious relief for asthma, diabetes, constipation, tuberculosis, gastric distress, sciatica, and some other illnesses with the simple repetition of his general autosuggestion.

Among world psychological researchers, Emile Coue's home soon became known as the famed Nancy School. And while much of its activity was focused on working with adults and school age children, another serious focus included their work with pregnant women and babies. These endeavors were generally entrusted to the capable hands of a Mademoiselle Kauffmant, who then managed the children's clinic. Emile Coue believed that the psychological development of anyone should ideally begin inside of their mother's womb. Pregnant women were taught the importance of providing their baby with the proper atmosphere for them to grow. Women were cautioned to avoid fractious, disturbing, or alcoholic situations. They were also taught how to persuasively talk, sing, read, play music, or just relax for their child's benefit. The mother's use of Emile Coue's general affirmation was then seen to encourage a relatively easy birth.

Afterwards, all mothers were taught the vital importance of continuing this activity, such that it might encourage their child's development in most every way. At night, they were encouraged to whisper loving assurances as the baby slept.

It is expected that they were introduced to Emile Coue's famous affirmations long before they ever knew the meaning of the words. Both parents were then taught to encourage and support them in every way imaginable. They were routinely taught that an ill child should always be lovingly held and massaged in a way that then eased any physical problem, while the parent then calmly repeated Emile Coue's reassuring affirmations.

It is important to note that Emile Coue personally saw his work as being strictly medical in nature, where the patients were taught how to help themselves. He did not see his practice as being at all religious or conflicting with anyone's religious affiliation. Emile Coue later became concerned that his work was possibly being exploited by some people pretending to be religious healers. He wanted everyone to know that he was most assuredly 'not' any such healer. He saw any healing that occurred as being accomplished by the very patients themselves.

Today, Emile Coue would probably be highly critical of all the late night radio and TV programs that now spread all sorts of wild ideas to people in such a highly suggestible psychological state. Insomnia is now a widespread problem that offers many potential victims for exploitive broadcasters. Their victims may be easily conned into donating money that they cannot afford, or in believing some of the wildest nonsense you could ever imagine.

Emile Coue saw himself as being a simple teacher of ancient truths offering a very practical therapy that could help people to put their lives in order and make the most out of their personal talents and aspirations. Over the years, he entertained thousands of eager students and patients in his large home and garden in the city of Nancy, situated in the heart of France. Since his death, that home has become a popular museum and educational center. His books and foreign tours made his work available to people all over the world. Some are still available on Ebay and Internet. Few people have left a more indelible mark on the world. Coue's affirmation is widely recited today, in many languages. And his cordial respectability may well offer us all a template for building new and valuable relationships around a world that is getting smaller every day.

REFLEXIVE FEEDBACK

The ability to communicate with your subconscious is invaluable in building a meaningful relationship. We have all had our own hunches and intuitive feelings. Professional hypnotists can even talk to our subconscious under hypnosis, but this offers little help in shaping your daily life. Our conscious and subconscious minds communicate in quite different manners. While the conscious mind commands our speaking ability, the subconscious mind controls our ideomotor reflexes. These subtle reflex motions are then controlled by the sympathetic portion of the autonomic nervous system, which also controls our fight or flight response. Any communication between your two minds requires that you then understand this fundamental situation and all of its obvious limitations. Given that, it can still offer you invaluable assistance in your self-improvement.

In 1933 the noted French chemist, Michel Chevreul, set out to expose the popular occult phenomena of rod and pendulum dowsing as a monumental fraud. Instead, he discovered that the pendulum facilitated direct practical communication with our subconscious via our ideomotor reflexes.

His Chevreul Pendulum is easily constructed using any small weight tied to about ten inches (25 cm) of heavy thread or fine metal chain as shown. Various pendulums are available on both eBay and Amazon, with their use demonstrated on YouTube.

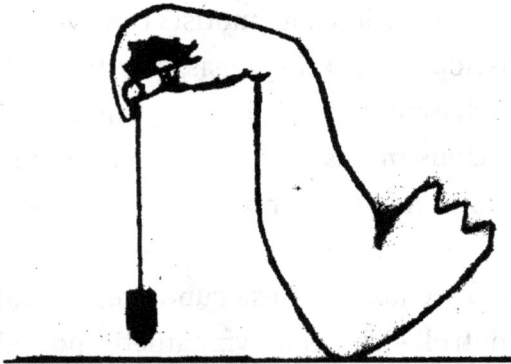

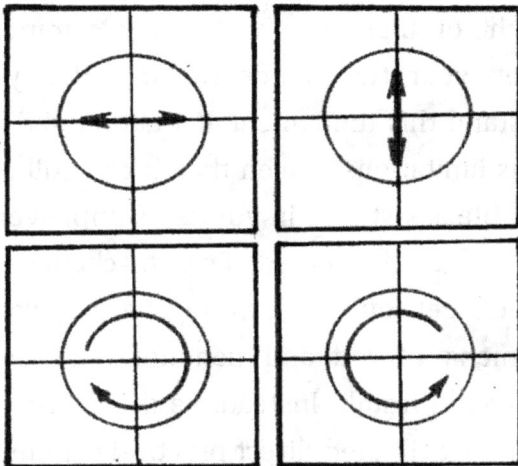

CHEVREUL PENDULUM OPERATION

ALIGN YOUR MINDS

The end of the string is held in your dominant hand, between the thumb and forefinger, with your elbow resting on a flat surface. A sheet of paper with a circle six inches (15 cm) in diameter and vertical and horizontal axes is placed under it. The pendulum can then be moved forward and backward, side to side, clockwise, or counter-clockwise by your subconscious mind. These will indicate YES, NO, DON'T KNOW or CAN'T TELL type responses. After relaxing alone, you begin by asking yourself, out loud, to please move the pendulum to indicate a YES response. Do not consciously try to make it move. Your own subconscious mind will eventually move the pendulum in one of the four ways. Note that response next to that illustration. After a clear response has been obtained, thank yourself and use your free hand to still the moving pendulum. Then, in a similar manner, ask your subconscious mind to demonstrate NO, DON'T KNOW, and CAN'T TELL type responses. Carefully note each one of these next to the appropriate illustration.

You must begin any interrogation by relaxing alone and endeavoring to still your mind of any distracting thoughts. Holding the pendulum as shown, ask yourself some initial questions to verify its integrity and potential to yourself. Ask it if your name is XXXXXX? See if it says NO to a knowingly false situation, like is this Monday, when it's Friday? After you are fully satisfied of its performance, you are ready to explore your specific interests. You will need to reduce everything to a sequence of very simple YES or NO type inquiries. Do not use any complex type sentences or phraseology.

You should not think simple YES and NO replies will ever seriously restrict your ability to question your subconscious mind. Quantitative type evaluations can be made just by asking it if something is bigger than something else, then another thing, until you have an idea of the size. A particular time can be isolated by asking if it happened before this year, then that year, until you isolate the right period. Such tactics can be readily designed to explore many interests. A CAN'T TELL type response may mean that there is some mental blockage occurring regarding some sensitive matter. It is always wise to ask key questions in multiple ways to be sure that your subconscious mind fully understands the particular question being asked.

Do not waste time asking about anything that is not actually logged into your personal history. Any response to a subjective type question should generally be considered as an intuitive hunch, and not necessarily a hard fact. Some typical potential inquiries may then include the following:

Finding Lost Items	**Physical Problems**
Friend Assessment	**Drugs/Supplements**
Examining Motives	**Dieting & Exercise**
Detection of Deceit	**Personal Investing**
Weighing Decisions	**Threat Assessment**
Exploring Memory	**Buy/Sell Decisions**
Location Appraisal	**Ideal Time & Place**
Medical Conditions	**Concealed Problems**
Health Provisions	**Education Choices**

Such expeditions into your own personal subconscious character can offer you a close look at your innermost feelings and experience. It is usually best to start out with simple objective studies, like finding that prized possession that you mislaid years ago. The sequence of questions may then begin by asking if you know what may have happened to it? Given a yes, ask if it is here, then there, until you zero in on some potential location. Of course, it could no longer still be there, if someone else may have already found it.

Some subjective investigations may involve assessing your personal relationship with someone. You might begin by asking if you have any special feelings regarding them? If the answer is yes, you may sequentially inquire if those feelings are positive, negative, affectionate, hopeful, supportive, fearful, etc? You will always want to proceed very carefully in order not to prejudice the response. Your results should always be considered intuitive. Subsequently, you might even like to propose taking some assertive action with that person in order to appraise the results. Ask yourself if you would do this or that, would you expect them to react negatively, positively, etc. until you have an idea of their suspected response. You might then even want to actually consider testing your investigative results in person.

Basic health and fitness are very natural concerns for everyone and your subconscious may have a lot to say about them. You might start by asking if some particular symptom being experienced is serious? If so, ask if it might be caused by this, or that, until you have some idea of what might be responsible. You might then ask if this or that treatment seems to be helping or hurting? Is this medicine or that treatment schedule really the best for me? *Please note that this process should never be seen as any substitute for your obtaining the appropriate professional medical advice.*

Many subtle environmental factors may well affect our subconscious comfort related to our own daily living and working conditions. Practitioners of some architectural philosophies, like Feng Shui, consider this important for our personal health and productivity. You might then ask if a particular place is good for you? Should your bed or desk then best be placed here or there? Could the situation then possibly be improved by making this or that adjustment?

Many marriages and business partnerships tend to fail due to some subtle underlying personality conflicts. To maximize your potential success, you might want to begin by exposing various aspects of yourselves to each other over an extended period. The pendulum may then be asked if this or that venture is truly compatible with your natural characters? You might then want to ask if this or that aspect of your personal relationship may be especially good, bad, or improvable somehow?

Your subconscious mind knows all of your important talents and inclinations. Their opinion should really matter when it comes to taking a vacation, pursuing an education, or seeking any employment. Various questions can be used to systematically explore them. You might start by reviewing your previous education and the subjects that you liked the most. You might also explore your varied personal needs and working experience. The individual aspects of your current options might then be carefully assessed until you feel assured of what you might like to explore further. You might also consider asking yourself if there is perhaps some special friend or associate that you should consult, due to their personal knowledge and appreciation of your own special background. Any thorough investigation of your personal future might be done best in conjunction with your gradual development of your anticipated planning on paper. This will then help you to systematically isolate any vital questions to explore.

WORLDLY EXPERIENCE

World literature contains many charming lullabies designed to ease children into a hopeful slumber. Most mothers have always seemed to understand the psychological importance of teaching children to sing or say some simple inspiring little ditty. Do you remember all those children's stories where the struggling heroes repeatedly say to themselves: I think I can? The words I am, I can, and I will are aspiring fundamental ideas that every child needs to be introduced to as early as possible, preferably inside their mother's womb. This is the foundation upon which autosuggestion research was built.

Television has made great children's programs, like Mister Rogers' Neighborhood and Sesame Street, available around the world. Programs that gave them hopeful outlooks, taught inspiring ideas, and songs to motivate their everyday lives. Inevitably, these learning experiences then helped us all to better deal with the many challenges in our lives.

The nature of our current times is a big factor in shaping the character of any emerging leaders. It was significant that Emile Coue's work was born out of direct personal experience in the midst of the first World War and the deadly Spanish Flu pandemic of 1918. One hundred years later, we found ourselves being victimized by an insidious new Russian form of hybrid warfare and our own COVID pandemic. These dual dilemmas were interwoven in a fashion that maximized their cost in both American lives and our national integrity.

Russia's leader, Vladimir Putin, launched his subtle new hybrid type of war in retaliation for the economic sanctions imposed for invading the Crimean Peninsula in 2014. The COVID pandemic was an accidental complication that dramatically affected America's national economy, civil society, public health, and world leadership. Together, they literally seemed to threaten the very existence of our democratic way of life.

Although autosuggestion had emerged out of World War I and the pandemic of 1918, it was built upon Emile Coue's long and patient research into the placebo effect. People everywhere had then needed a practical way to rebuild their personal lives while they struggled to deal with all of the mental, emotional and physical demands of their trying times. Autosuggestion's profound success was rooted in its utter simplicity and practical effectiveness with all sorts of people and problems. Our modern world could surely use that help today. However, today's complex and chaotic American society poses many new and daunting challenges.

Coue's work on the placebo effect had focused his attention on understanding the powerful role played by our subconscious. His pharmacy in Troyes, France, had served thousands of people of all ages, sexes, classes, and professions. He had personally seen that the psychological placebo effect didn't really matter if you were rich or poor, educated or illiterate. While some people clearly required more skill than others to assure them of the appropriateness of using any given medicine, the results were often the same, independent of whether the treatment itself was any good at all. Emile Coue had discovered the phenomenal fact that our subconscious mind literally constitutes the simple trusting side of us all. He then came to believe that our proper understanding of just how our subconscious mind actually works was essential to making the most out of life.

I often hear that autosuggestion is too simplistic to be of real significance to any educated person. I used to think that too. Emile Coue then clearly changed my mind. Many research scientists, like me, have often found themselves to be working alone, unfunded, and despairing of any proper support in their devoted innovative undertakings. It is then a major challenge to figure out how you can even survive long enough to accomplish your objectives.

In my case, I had long been interested in the power of self-hypnotism to help people focus their energy on getting ahead. However, my ventures into this realm always ended in disappointment, probably due to my left brain type character causing me too much internal resistance. I then started looking into the history of applied psychology. Emile Coue in France, and Sigmund Freud in Austria, were colleagues in the same era. While Freud served the sophisticated interests of medical professionals in developing psychoanalysis, Coue sought to serve the practical needs of a general audience that was desperate for assistance. Although psychoanalysis clearly has invaluable uses, it is often just too demanding, takes too long, and is far too costly for most everyday needs. Emile Coue saw that many of the people around him needed help right then and there. The crowded scenes in his home and garden clearly endorsed his view.

His great results then spoke for themselves. However, to fully understand Emile Coue's success, I would like to invite everyone to take a closer look at his now world famous general affirmation:

Every day, in every way,
I am getting better and better.

This is not just some simple declarative sentence. I believe Emile Coue saw the need for a common mantra, emphasizing the words *I am*, that offered everyone a really easy way of bonding with their subconscious mind. One that could then help to unleash their own personal potential. Its spoken or silent recitation offered them a very real way to over-write all of their old destructive habits and introduce a new subconscious perspective.

His practice was then generally focused on helping patients overcome some medical problem. He helped them appreciate the importance of vocal repetition on getting their subconscious mind's attention. Whether you sought improved health or attaining another objective, Coue helped people master control of their two minds. This was like the invigoration a runner feels when they get their second wind, and think they could run forever.

Thomas E. Loxley

While repetition is one way to impress your subconscious mind, adding emotional emphasis is another fundamental way we can denote special information for future retrieval. You don't have to introduce painful physical trauma to do this. All you really need to do is to clap your hands. Coupling that information, sound, and impact can help note its importance to your subconscious mind. You'd be surprised just how many people use such simple tricks to help them to remember big ideas.

Many people have been well advised to sleep on a difficult problem in the hope of having a better perspective in the morning. Artists have often found that their current work suddenly comes into proper focus after a good night's rest. Creative designers, of all sorts, have awoken to find they suddenly knew just how to fit everything together to meet some challenging requirements. Music composers, like Wolfgang Mozart, have awaken to find themselves laying out whole symphonies, that just poured forth. In olden times, such dreams and critical experiences were often attributed to having communicated with the gods. Emile Coue's work then showed us all how we could best use our own subconscious minds while we slept.

Many have trouble taking written exams. They get tense and nervous and seem to have trouble recalling knowledge they knew they had. That problem can often be made to then disappear, if on the previous night they just sought the help of their subconscious mind. Just before going to sleep, they simply needed to review the test requirements and visualize themselves passing it. Their subconscious mind will then often work all night long just to make that goal a reality.

The evolution of modern autosuggestion has now led to the organized assembly of all of the considerations that were introduced earlier. Our subconscious suggestibility is naturally greater when we enter an alpha brain state. This is something we can induce simply by relaxing and closing our eyes, but is better done just before and after sleeping. This ability can then be cultivated by practicing mindfulness. Mindfulness generally relates to the shifting of your mental focus to obtain relief from some stressful living situation. We are then urged to refocus our total attention inward on our own rhythmic breathing, or our beating heart, as a mental refuge from the chaos raging all around us. I often seek a similar escape into some attractive natural setting, where I can then get lost in the surrounding scenery. Watching the clouds moving across the sky, the waves on the river, the breeze moving through the trees, or the local wildlife activity can then help me to mentally get away. This vital stress relief could well save your life.

An ability to clearly visualize your objective is really critical in focusing your subconscious thinking on its fulfillment. In order to cultivate this capability, people have concocted a variety of simple mental aids. Many writers create mock covers for their new book, which they then prop up on their desk while they write it. Architects will make up scale models of any buildings they are designing. Engineers often devise movable models of potential devices. And many artists will surround themselves with photos of the subjects that they wish to portray. The more vividly that you can depict your desires, the more effective your subconscious concentration will be.

The use of the Chevreul Pendulum can offer you a jarring realization of your own independent subconscious personality. That realization should then be utilized to build a mutual appreciation of your own conscious and subconscious differences.

This should then be utilized to build mutual understanding and cooperation. No one can really solve a personal problem if they don't understand the nature of its existence. Reflex communication with your subconscious mind can then help you to do just that. Indeed, it is one of your most vital tools.

Life itself is now literally your own personal laboratory for developing the relationship between your conscious and subconscious minds. The first order of business might then be to consider how to handle all the accumulating personal information. When your conscious, short term memory, no longer requires some particular information, how should your subconscious, long term memory, deal with it? A professional secretary would set up a formal filing system, labeling each one so that they could readily retrieve anything whenever they needed it. How might your own memories then be properly organized to provide for their effective retrieval? Librarians routinely arrange their book shelves according to the Dewey Decimal Classification System, shown as follows in an abbreviated form. This popular system breaks down all of the various subject matters into areas that are numerically listed from 000 to 999.

DEWEY DECIMAL SYSTEM

---

000   **Computer science & general work**
100   **Philosophy & psychology**
200   **Religion**
300   **Social sciences**
400   **Language**
500   **Science**
600   **Technology**
700   **Arts & recreation**
800   **Literature**
900   **History & geography**

This book is listed under 158 Applied Psychology. Could we possibly learn how to then categorize our thoughts in ways that might aid in their retrieval? If we started using such categories at an early age, could it help our sleeping subconscious mind to easily seek out any information when we needed it? Indeed, could this faculty potentially streamline our mental retrieval processes so that our subconscious mind doesn't have to search through everything at night just to answer some specific question? Moreover, could this capability then conceivably increase what scientists properly call our personal *Intelligence Quotient*, abbreviated as *IQ*?

ALIGN YOUR MINDS

No two people are identical in regard to their nature, needs, or aspirations. Their best practice of autosuggestion should always accommodate that uniqueness to its benefit. The value of this can be seen in the careers of many great comedians. Most of them have used any humorous aspects of their childhood, appearance, love life, relatives, religion, etc. to tickle a good laugh out of their audience. While we all may have any number of reasons to be bitter about some past experiences, why let it destroy yourself when humor offers its own revenge, if you use it to motivate your success. We all need to learn how to laugh at ourselves so that we might effectively convert the inevitable lemons in all of our lives into some lemonade.

I propose that everyone needs to consider using their special talents or interests to accent their everyday life and the use of autosuggestion in promoting their own wellness and aspirations. This can take on many forms, depending upon your special talents, background, and situation. You might create your own motto to live by, a coat of arms, theme song, artistic signature, hair style, dance step, dress code, or most anything that can then remind you of your aspirations.

The challenge is to visualize yourself weaving everything into an aspiring life story that fires up your imagination and desire to actually live the life of your own creation. Needless to say, questions of its practical feasibility may arise, but these can always usually be adjusted somehow. The big thing to remember is that your own aspirations can potentially open opportunities that you probably never envisioned and should be given an adequate chance to materialize. Moreover, your ability to design a life that you might like to enjoy can provoke your research into its feasibility, and help you to map out all of the steps needed to make it actually come true.

One of the first steps in anyone's quest to do almost anything should be to gather all of the available information on what you want to do. That is a whole lot easier to do today, thanks to our public libraries and the worldwide Internet. Most libraries now even offer free computers for you to use as well as training courses on how to use them and how to find almost anything that you need to know. Indeed, they can literally help you to isolate any key sources or individuals that might well be critical to your personal success.

PERSONAL DEVELOPMENT

The true power and impact of Emile Coue's work is that it offers everyone a practical down-to-earth opportunity to become a master of their two minds. There are no abstract psychological theories or complex analysis techniques involved. Although many use autosuggestion on a short term basis to treat specific problems, others then see it as a long term, fundamental, part of their everyday lives. Long term users see a natural evolution of their experience as the extended repetition of Coue's basic affirmation becomes less and less necessary to get their subconscious mind's attention.

It seems to become progressively easier to slip into a suggestive state when we go to bed at night. This is almost like our subconscious mind seems to be anticipating our latest request for what might be explored that night. It is often substantiated by our new perspective on the subject, when we wake up the following day. Moreover, as we learn how to better visualize our desires, it is often reflected in our morning realization of its serious consideration. There is a growing sense of comerraderie between our two minds, as if our subconscious mind believes it is finally getting the appreciation that it deserves. This creates a subtle sense of personal satisfaction.

The realization of any sense of self mastery over your two minds is akin to a growing feeling of being at peace with just who you are. You just seem to know that somehow, together, you can probably deal well with almost anything that comes along. But, more than this, you feel open to expanding your world in new ways that can help you feel like your outlook, talents, and capabilities are growing. You feel like you are constantly improving your options for tackling anything that comes along. And that is a really good feeling for anyone to have.

Having grown up in the 1940s, with no money to spare, I was encouraged to constantly explore any options to improve my situation. Over the years, this created a sense of satisfaction that I could usually figure out a way ahead. I was blessed never to suffer from the depression that now seems to haunt so many people today. I believe that my diverse childhood activities may well have played a major role. My project oriented lifestyle meant that there was always another exciting thing to do. And every project opened the door to meeting other people who were as dynamic and committed as me.

I am now 83 years old and still physically active, constantly learning and doing new things.

I would encourage everyone to consider how they too might best expand their personal horizons. I'm always looking for a skyline or scenic vista that stirs my imagination. My inveterate sky watching has caused me to be forever facinated with clouds and sunsets during the day, and the moon and stars at night. I feel great when my body still seems to be capable of striding right along on my daily walks. Have you ever noticed how your whole experience often seems to be different when you change your perspective on anything? Are you really being observant and appreciative of life itself and the world around you? All our lives are truly the integrated summation of millions and millions of little actions and observations. Together, they are what life's satisfaction and happiness are all about. Taken step by step by step, every life then offers opportunities for all of us to make each day another step forward as well as our world a better place. This can then naturally evolve into a sense of your very own mission in life. One that is bigger than yourself alone. I can personally credit Emile Coue with helping to do precisely that for me.

Thomas E. Loxley

RESEARCH APPLICATION

This book is based on the direct application of these long proven techniques in support of my own engineering research done in the modern world. All scientist's dream of making some big discovery. However, the world is not noted for welcoming them with open arms, especially when they seemed to be challenging the established economic order. As an engineering scientist, my work has focused on exploring new perspectives on solving some of our oldest problems. In 1977, I set my sights on changing the way that we heat and cool our homes and its role in our current global warming dilemma.

In this quest, I came upon basic geophysical research done in the 1960s, in the geothermal area of New Zealand. Dr. John W. Elder showed that a natural stimulation of a slow convective circulation of moisture in the ground could literally amplify its normal upward heat transfer, over geothermal hot spots, by 100,000-times. The upward velocity of the moisture itself was estimated to only be about ten millimeters per hour. This discovery had effectively explained the odd heat transfer effects seen in many geothermal areas around the world.

Any related moisture movement in the ground could represent a similar heat transfer opportunity, all be it at a much lower temperature differential. My attention turned to the common form of upward moisture movement in the ground that is known as rising damp. This is an upward capillary movement of soil moisture. It is motivated simply by covering the ground surface with a flat rock, concrete slab, or plastic sheeting. Many builders see rising damp as a real menace, causing widespread building decay and unwanted heat loss. One of its most effective solutions was developed in Scotland, where they started building homes on top of plastic diaphragms. These were formed by pouring molten coal tar on top of prepared ground, covering the entire site. It not only kept out rising damp, but also any radon gas coming from underground mineral deposits. Similar homes built in adjacent areas of England and Scotland showed serious radon problems in England, and none in Scotland.

If sufficient ground is covered by a diaphragm, it will naturally affect the moisture distribution in the soil under it. This effect can then be enlarged vertically if we just extend the outer perimeter downward in the form of a continuous exterior skirt that etends below the local frost penetration depth. Adding sufficient insulation, to the top and sides of this plastic diaphragm, offers to bring the local subsoil temperature up to the surface in winter. This effect could be maximized by any induced convective circulation of the moisture as shown. Soil science data showed a feasibility of obtaining a stable heat flow of 40 to 50 watts per square meter.

❶ SOIL MOISTURE IS MAXIMIZED BY A SKIRTED PLASTIC MEMBRANE CAP.

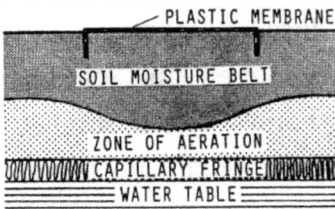

PLASTIC MEMBRANE

SOIL MOISTURE BELT

ZONE OF AERATION

CAPILLARY FRINGE

WATER TABLE

❷ SUBSOIL TEMPERATURE BROUGHT TO SURFACE BY ADDING INSULATION.

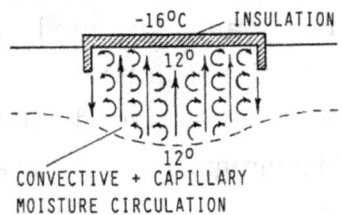

$-16^{\circ}C$ — INSULATION

12°

12°

CONVECTIVE + CAPILLARY MOISTURE CIRCULATION

GROUND COVER EFFECTS

We wanted to see if this might offer low-rise buildings, having an extended insulation envelope, that would thermally behave like caves. In 1978, the 2-story, 223 m^2 (2400 ft^2), test home shown was built in the eastern panhandle of West Virginia. It repeatedly demonstrated stable temperatures of 12°C (54°F) downstairs and 11°C (52°F) upstairs, with -16°C (4°F) outside, and no heating equipment.

INVERTED CAVE TEST HOME

Standard heating systems have a big flaw. They are assumed the only source of heat lost through the floor, walls and ceiling. This theory encourages the use of oversize equipment and high energy costs. Most builders like it because it is simple to install.

CONVENTIONAL SYSTEM

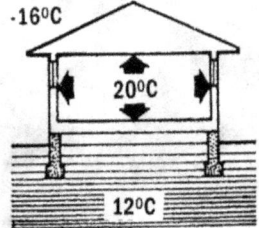

The inverted cave shatters this myth using an extended insulation envelope to tap 40 W/m² of heat from the ground. An induced soil moisture circulation carries the subsoil temperature into home. It needs little more heat in winter and is naturally cool in summer.

BASIC INVERTED CAVE

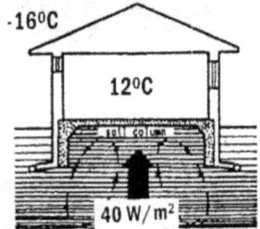

Full system adds water storage and circulation loop under floor. A water-to-air heat pump yields 4-times the performance of a resistance heater. In cold areas, small wall-mounted solar collector boosts soil temperature. This has reduced heating costs up to 95%.

FULL INVERTED CAVE SYSTEM

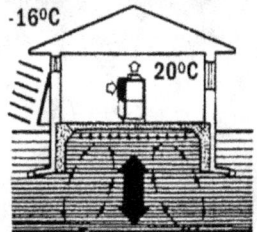

INVERTED CAVE PHENOMENON

The full inverted cave heating and cooling system shown uses a water-to-air electric heat pump and modest, wall-mounted, solar collector with the serpentine water storage and circulation loop. This recorded 'annual' heating costs as low as $50 for heating to 20°C (68°F). This was actually less power than was consumed by the average American kitchen refrigerator. The energy savings then paid back the added construction costs in only two years. The professional documentation of both the home construction and performance repeatedly attested to both its scientific integrity and wide potential use.

Most anyone might have expected such research to have then won serious governmental support. Yet, its novel perspective and ground-coupled home performance assessment caused such support to be politically suppressed. It seemingly challenged the corporate control of U.S. home construction and the established engineering dogma on the building insulation envelope design. My first peer reviewed paper was for a National Bureau of Standards conference in 1980 on the important issue of Building Energy Performance Standards (BEPS). This portrayed the inverted cave phenomenon as representing a *Self-Inspecting Home of the Future.'*

All Heating Equipment is OFF.
Local Subsoil Temperature is 54°F.
Average Outside Air Temperature is 15°F.

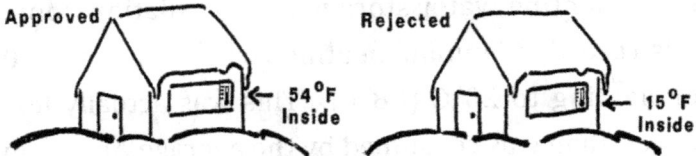

Approved ← 54°F Inside   Rejected ← 15°F Inside

THE SELF-INSPECTING HOME

The imposing of any building performance standards in America was highly controversial. And the inverted cave phenomenon was now seen as a new and most insidious form of BEPS. Builders dreaded they might be burdened with a two-step design procedure. The first to design a new extended type insulation envelope to tap the subsoil heating potential, and the second step to design its supplemental comfort control. If they didn't do it right, the winter temperature inside, with all of the heating equipment shut off, would show everyone if they knew what they were doing.

Ronald Reagan's presidential campaign declared that the ongoing energy crisis was an utter hoax. He promised that he would put a stop to BEPS, and any related research, if he was elected. As a result, he won the support of America's builders and the presidency. He immediately shut down all of the funding for the Center for Building Technology at the National Bureau of Standards, which was then developing BEPS, and any related activity, like mine. This then made me and my work persona non grata, in spite of its proven energy savings, and its major environmental significance. In the blink of an eye, I had unknowingly become an unperson in America.

Ronald Reagan had long been the public spokesman for the General Electric Corporation before going into politics. Accordingly, he had clearly developed a natural fondness for America's corporate CEO's and the national leadership that they provided. This personal bias was a big part of his presidency. He seemed to have little comprehension of the different roles played by science and technology in shaping our society. While its corporations exploited any 'patentable' technology for the development of profitable new business ventures, scientific progress was often focused on deciphering the various basic phenomena that then govern our natural world. The inverted cave phenomenon had illustrated how a natural upward mass transfer of the moisture in the ground could mobilize the solar energy, stored in the local subsoil, and transmit it up into an above grade building envelope. This was not patentable and its development had depended on the normal avenues of governmental and academic support. As the American government became increasingly controlled by corporate lobbyists, they aggressively sought to restrict any scientific discoveries that they saw as a threat to their market domination. Ronald Reagan clearly had no comprehension of the value of our scientific discovery and acted to serve the natural interests of his own corporate heros, blocking any perceived threats to their profitability.

It left many scientists, like myself, on our own and uncertain of our survival, with little objective support for developing our big discoveries into practice for their proper use by American society. Some may actually see this as the covert economic nazification of capitalism. While racist German Nazism robbed, raped and murdered its way in the world using bombs, bullets, and cyanide, America's super capitalists did it all economically, using the Almighty Dollar to then purloin resources, impose product dependency, and regulate any employment compensation to suit its greed-driven executives.

This may be the only way to interpret the fond relations between Wall Street and Adolf Hitler that existed prior to World War II. It just replaced an ugly race war, with a semi-colonial economic one.

As a scientist, I felt morally obligated to put my discovery before the world in a manner befitting its importance. I hopefully figured that, along the way, I might somehow acquire the support required. But, I was one man working with limited resources in a time when my home mortgage rates had risen to a brutal twelve percent. The test home evalution included a 3-year, 10-phase, step-by-step appraisal of the inverted cave effect, plus the addition of the heat pump, solar array, and auxilary woodstove. The home's heating and cooling performance were appraised, along with dozens of contributing design variables. Fourteen technical papers have been published as we sought to define the contents of the official *Inverted Cave Handbook*, shown on page 84. In 1993 our one-man operation had been seriously jeopardized by coronary artery disease. My gradual, impoverished recovery then made the use of autosuggestion critical in all of the tasks involved. Night after night, every detail had to be dealt with. The handbook is now finally nearing its publication.

THE INVERTED CAVE HANDBOOK
Thomas E. Loxley
General Contents

In 2022 we published *'Global Warming Reality: A Naturalist Action Plan'* as a major public warning. It sought to educate everyone about the importance of dealing with the increasing solar energy that is now being stored in the ground due to our ever expanding population and real estate development. It seeks to show how the inverted cave phenomenon offers a real opportunity to turn the solar energy stored underground into a vital new heat source. The *Insulated Pad Test Exhibit,* shown below, is now being promoted to help people around the world to see for themselves just how the inverted cave phenomenon might work in their area. It consists of a 6-mil polyethylene ground cover, a 4-inch layer of extruded polystyrene foam insulation, and a polypropylene tarpaulin that's staked to level ground.

Display shows temperature under center of a 16-foot square plastic foam insulation pad 4-inches thick. It illustrates local capability of an upwelling capillary moisture to bring up heat from deep underground. This base temperature might then be available to an above grade home using *Inverted Cave* phenomenon.

$12^\circ C\ (54^\circ F)$

INSULATION PAD TEST EXHIBIT

CONCLUSIONS

Emile Coue's enormous motivational impact was very clearly based on his carefully crafted general autosuggestion being repeated just before sleeping. This offers you a powerful new way of realigning your subconscious thinking in a positive fashion. It deals directly with the dilemma facing those who go to bed with their heads still roiling with all of the stress and concerns of their busy working day. This can then cause them to spend all night in a destructive frame of mind that offers little rest. Emile Coue believed you could breathe hope into your life just repeating his general autosuggestion. You really do owe it to yourself to just give it a try. It should be done daily for at least a week. You might even like repeating it at any time you want.

Everyone needs to appreciate the importance of cultivating a good relationship with their own subconscious mind. While rote learning may now be out of vogue with many educators, it is really a fundamental way of shaping your subconscious mind to your own best interests. Your peace of mind is dependent upon your realizing that fact. Moreover, such simple straight forward types of remedies are generally the best ones when you are working with human nature.

Emile Coue's general autosuggestion has stood the test of time and it should be a part of everyone's personal survival kit. As an engineering scientist, I am a proud supporter of Emile Coue's approach. Whenever my friends ask me how I am doing, I like to say: *"Better and better."* This always reminds me of how he has really helped me better understand and work with my own subconscious self. Indeed, you can always count on them being around whenever you really need them most.

When it comes to self-improvement techniques, you can't beat the inexpensive effectiveness of Emile Coue's assistance. It had used to be freely available at most public libraries. His modern competitors can't be expected to appreciate him outperforming their expensive or ineffective work. Just compare autosuggestion with the high cost and long years now involved with psychoanalysis, which only succeeds with about one in four people. A good hypnotherapist is often more successful. Popular motivational coaches, like Anthony Robbins, are available. And Tony might even offer you the opportunity of walking barefoot over hot coals.

Today, many good motivational speakers also offer inexpensive audio and video programs. Several excellent videos are now available on YouTube.

The authorities cited in this work, Emile Coue and Michel Chevreul, were both French. While the Scandinavians love nature, Germans engineering, and English literature, the people of France really see themselves as fine connoisseurs of life itself. The country has been central to many historic developments in both the fine arts and humanities. They deeply value good friends, home creation, fine cuisine, healthy living, romantic love, raising children, and great art as something to be savored. I would like to thank them for giving us these men. Their great work may offer some vital help to an America that is now being needlessly devastated by mass shootings and drug overdose deaths.

As David Riesman's other directed people grow older, they are often set adrift when the dominating people in their lives are gone. I encourage everyone to develop a personal interest in project oriented activities. That way, no matter what, they might always find joy and satisfaction in doing something they really like to do, and can do with future friends. This has been a real lifesaver for me.

BIBLIOGRAPHY

1. Coue, Emile *Self Mastery Through Conscious Autosuggestion*, American Library Service, New York 1922.

2. Coue, Emile *My Method: Including American Impressions*, Doubleday, Page & Company, Garden City, NY 1923.

3. Baudouin, C. *Suggestion and Autosuggestion: A Psychological and Pedagogical Study Based on the Investigations made by the New Nancy School*, George Allen & Unwin Ltd., London 1920.

4. Brooks, C. Harry *The Practice of Autosuggestion by the Method of Emile Coue*, George Allen & Unwin Ltd., London 1922.

5. Orton, J. L. *Hypnotism Made Practical*, Thorsons Publishers Ltd., London 1955.

6. Hudson, Thomas J. *The Law of Psychic Phenomena: A Working Hypothesis*, Hudson-Cohan Publishing Company, Salinas, CA 1977.

7. Lecron, Leslie M. *Self Hypnosis: The Technique and its Use in Daily Living*, Prentice-Hall, Inc., Englewood Cliffs, NJ 1964.

8. Tebbetts, Charles *Self-Hypnosis and Other Mind-Expanding Techniques*, Westwood Publishing Company, Inc., Glendale, CA 1987.

9. Chips, Allen, *Clinical Hypnotherapy: A Transpersonal Approach*, Transpersonal Publishing, Goshen, VA 2004.

10. Powers, Melvin *Encyclopedia of Self Hypnotism*, Improvement Books Co., Opa Locka, FL 1975.

11. Barrett, W. & T. Besterman *The Divining Rod*, University Books, New Hyde Park, NY 1968.

12. Welch, Bryant *State of Confusion: Political Manipulation and the Assault on the American Mind*, Thomas Divine Books, St. Martin's Press, New York 2008.

13. Elder, John W. *Geothermal Systems*, Academic Press, London 1981.

14. Loxley, Thomas E. Article: *'Inverted Cave' House* in Building Research & Practice, The Journal of CIB, Jan-Feb 1985, Paris, p. 13-20.

Thomas E. Loxley

ABOUT THE AUTHOR

Thomas E. Loxley is a 1961 graduate of the innovative Engineering Science R&D program at Case Institute of Technology. He studied thermodynamics under Dr. Jerzy Moszynski, a noted authority on multiple heat source systems. He is a former U.S. Navy scientist and Virginia Tech professor listed in *American Men of Science* and classified Mechanical Engineer, General Engineer and Physicist by the U.S. Civil Service. He coauthored *U.S. Energy Policy Game* and led Virginia energy conservation. His inverted cave research into tapping the solar energy stored in the Earth's surface involved membership in the International Council for Building Research Studies and Documentation (CIB) and its W67 Working Commission on Energy Conservation in the Built Environment. W67 papers were published in Sweden in 87, Austria in 88, France in 89, Germany in 90, and Norway in 91. Plus others in CIB World Congress Proceedings in Washington in 86 and Paris in 89, CIB Journal in 85 and 92, the National Bureau of Standards in 81, U.S. Solar Energy Society in 82, Sweden's North Sun Conference in 88, UK World Renewable Energy Congress in 90, and IEA World Conference in 93. Other work included investigating deadly Vietnam War weapon failures, longwall mine hydraulic roof supports, patenting new test instrumentation, eliminating major shipboard hazard, helping build Pisces deep-diving submersibles. Selected for the Peace Corps, elected precinct Judge of Elections. Traveled widely, hiking Austria and Ireland. Survived open heart surgery, COVID, etc. Recent books now include *Align Your Minds,* promoting self-improvement, and the timely essays *Global Warming Reality* and *America's Manifest Destiny.* He is now finalizing a major handbook on his inverted cave research. Inactive on social media, he lives on Ohio River in Beaver, PA.

GLOBAL WARMING REALITY
A Naturalist Action Plan

Thomas E. Loxley

Global warming is a direct result of Earth's solar absorption exceeding its ability to dissipate that heat into space. Some exploitive politicians want you to think this is all just some simple matter of excess atmospheric greenhouse gases suppressing Earth's natural heat dissipation rate. While some regional production of greenhouse gases have slightly declined, the overall release of both CO_2 and methane have been steadily increasing. Moreover, no effort to speed up its dissipation can succeed as long as the absorption rate is constantly growing due to our expanding human population, with all of the land development and energy consumption that it entails. This process seems tailor made to soak up ever more solar radiation. The outer twenty meters (66 feet) of the Earth's surface constitutes one huge solar collector. Modern industry has created global warming by wantonly destroying the vital insulative effect that was provided by the enormous forest canopy that had once shielded much of the Earth's surface from the Sun's direct radiation. We are now irresponsibly driving many of Earth's most magnificent lifeforms rapidly into extinction. The very survival of human civilization now depends upon our working together to immediately increase the solar reflectivity of the planet's surface in order to buy the time needed to restore the forest canopy that we wantonly destroyed.

Paperback and Ebook available on Internet

Thomas E. Loxley

AMERICA'S MANIFEST DESTINY
How History Haunts U.S. Conservation Leadership

Thomas E. Loxley

SUMMARY

America has seen a destructive politization of its scientific concerns dealing with critical issues such as energy and the environment. This has represented a desire by some powerful special interests to restrict technological evolution so that it only perpetuated their dominant position. Aggressive lobbying obstructed fair competition and restricted any government support to their selfish benefit. Their power to actually control this situation has now undermined its democracy and represents a growing national dysfunction that is very dangerously affecting the American role in the world. The roots of this dilemma are traced to a relentless perpetuation of Manifest Destiny, a philosophy which had been the driving force in colonial America. This exploitive psychological addiction has proven to be impossible to control. It is producing a pervasive national hypocrisy that defiles any hope of it ever being a rational democracy. Study of our population growth, resource depletion, consumptive lifestyles and evolving leadership illustrates today's vital need for a dynamic new renaissance in international altruism.

Paperback and Ebook Available on Internet

92

www.ingramcontent.com/pod-product-compliance
Lightning Source LLC
Chambersburg PA
CBHW050543280326
41933CB00011B/1707